How Artists View Homes

Karen Hosack

Heinemann Library
Chicago, Illinois

© 2005 Heinemann Library
a division of Reed Elsevier Inc.
Chicago, Illinois

Customer Service 888-454-2279
Visit our website at www.heinemannlibrary.com

Designed by Ron Kamen and Celia Floyd
Illustrations by Jo Brooker
Originated by Dot Gradations Ltd
Printed and bound in China by South China Printing Company

09 08 07 06 05
10 9 8 7 6 5 4 3 2 1

Library of Congress Cataloging-in-Publication Data
Hosack, Karen.
  Homes / Karen Hosack.
    v. cm. -- (How artists view)
  Includes index.
  Contents: How artists see homes -- Shape and tone -- Shapes and patterns -- Shapes and spaces -- Drawing different types of homes -- Distance and perspective -- Looking through doors -- Color and mood -- Murals -- Fantasy rooms -- Homes and gardens -- Clean your room! -- Your neighborhood.
  ISBN 1-4034-4853-1
  1. Dwellings in art--Juvenile literature. 2. Art--Juvenile literature. [1. Dwellings in art. 2. Art appreciation.] I. Title. II. Series.
  N8217.D94H67 2004
  704.9'44--dc22
                                        2003026361

Acknowledgments
The author and publisher are grateful to the following for permission to reproduce copyright material:

Art Archive pp. 9 (Paul Klee © DACS 2004), 20 (Bibliothèque des Arts Décoratifs, Paris / Dagli Orti); Bridgeman Art Library pp. 4 (The National Gallery, London), 15 (© ADAGP, Paris and DACS, London 2004), 18 (The Hermitage Museum, St Petersburg, Russia), 19 (Musee d.Orsay, Paris, France), 21 (Palais du Luxembourg, Paris), 24 (The National Gallery London); Corbis pp. 8, 10, 11 (David Glover), 23; Mary Evans Picture Library p. 26; The National Gallery, London pp. 14, 16; Ohara Museum of Art, Japan pp. 6, 28; Peter Evans p. 13 top; © Salvador Dali, Gala-Salvador Dali Foundation, DACS, London 2004 p. 22; Statens Museum for Kunst, Copenhagen p. 27; Tate London 2004 pp. 5 (Lowry Estate), 7 top (© Carl Andre / VAGA, New York / DACS, London 2004), 25; Tudor Photography pp. 13 middle, 13 bottom, 17 x 3, 29.

Cover photograph (*Curious Weather* by Mark Copeland, 1999) reproduced with permission of Portal Gallery London/Bridgeman Art Library.

Some words are shown in bold, **like this.** You can find out what they mean by looking in the glossary.

Contents

How Artists See Homes

An Autumn Landscape with a View of Het Steen in the Early Morning by Peter Paul Rubens, 1636

A home is a place where people live. Many artists enjoy painting the places where people live. Artist Peter Rubens painted this picture showing his own home. It looks like a castle! Rubens' home is set in the middle of beautiful countryside.

Painter L. S. Lowry enjoyed **sketching** the factories and workers' cottages in his hometown of Manchester, England. He used simple box shapes for the houses. He painted the people using lines. Lowry showed how tiny the people were compared to their homes and the huge smoking chimneys.

Industrial Landscape by L. S. Lowry, 1955

Shape and Tone

This artist has painted these houses using simple shapes. Notice how details like windows and doors have been left out. The artist has not drawn any of the bricks or tiles on the roofs. The houses look **three-dimensional** because different **tones** have been used for each side of the shapes.

Riverside Houses by Seiji Chokai, 1954

Carl Andre used ordinary house bricks to make this **sculpture.** He used the simple block shapes to create a larger rectangle on the floor. Such a simple sculpture makes us look at the shape and **texture** of the materials.

Equivalent VIII by Carl Andre, 1966

Make your own three-dimensional shape

You will need:

- *a pencil*
- *a piece of paper*

unshaded cube

shaded cube

Instructions:

1. Make a copy of the unshaded cube above.
2. Using a pencil, practice making different tones of grey.
3. Shade in the sides of the cube using different tones. This will make it look three-dimensional.

Shapes and Patterns

Egon Schiele put much detail into this picture. The patterns made by the roof tiles, bricks, and windows merge with the patterns made by the drying laundry. The shapes of the shirts and dresses on the clothesline make us think about the people who own them.

House with Drying Laundry by Egon Schiele, 1917

8

Architecture Spatiale by Paul Klee, 1915

The pattern in this painting is made by the colored squares used for the houses. It looks a bit like a **patchwork.** The painting is very flat because **tone** has not been used to show the sides of the houses. Some of the shapes are laid on top of each other. This makes the scene feel like a busy, modern town.

Shapes and Spaces

The people who design buildings are called **architects.** When architects design homes they think about the sort of things people use their houses for. Architect Le Corbusier designed homes that look like large, white solid shapes. The spaces inside these shapes are huge. Le Corbusier liked the idea of rooms flowing into each other, so he did not use many inside walls or doors. This is called an open-plan design.

Villa Savoye at Poissy, France, designed by Le Corbusier, 1928–1929

This is a **sculpture** of a house that was designed in **Victorian** times. Many families would have lived in the house over a period of about 150 years. In 1993, artist Rachel Whiteread filled the house with **plaster** to make a cast of the inside. After the plaster dried she took down all the outside walls. Can you see any similarities between the white shapes of this sculpture and the home on page ten?

Drawing Different Types of Homes

In the **fifteenth century,** an **architect** and painter named Leon Battista Alberti invented a viewfinder tool to help him draw. An artist looks through a frame like the one at the bottom of page thirteen, and draws what can be seen through it onto graph paper.

Make your own Alberti square

You will need:

- *a piece of cardboard approximately 4.7 in. x 4.7 in. (12 cm x 12 cm)*
- *a craft knife—you MUST ask an adult to help you use this*
- *a pencil*
- *black thread*
- *adhesive tape*
- *a ruler*

Instructions:

1. Make the cardboard into a frame by carefully cutting a 3.5 in. x 3.5 in. (9 cm x 9 cm) hole in the center. You should ask an adult to help you with this.

2. Using your pencil, measure and mark 1 in. (3 cm) and 2.3 in. (6 cm) along each side of the hole.

3. Make a small slit in the cardboard where you have placed the marks.

4. Cut four pieces of thread 4.3 in. (11 cm) long.

Using your Alberti square

Instructions:

1. First draw a nine-square grid on a piece of paper. Next, hold up your Alberti square in front of a house or other building that you would like to draw. You do not need to draw whole buildings. Instead, focus on interesting areas like patterns made by bricks, or shapes made by windows and doors.

2. Copy what you can see through the frame, square by square, on to your paper grid. You should now have your finished drawing!

5. Place the ends of the thread into the slits to make a grid of nine squares on the frame. Tape down the ends of each piece of thread. You should now have your finished viewfinder.

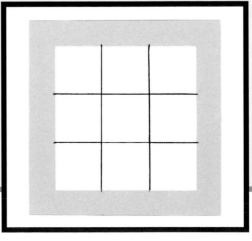

13

Distance and Perspective

Saint Jerome in his Study by Antonello da Messina, 1475–1476

The **Renaissance** was a time when many artists painted pictures that looked like views through a window. In this painting we are looking through a window at Saint Jerome in his study. The scene reaches far back into the room and even out through the windows in the distance. The way artists show things in the distance is called **perspective.**

The Window by Marc Chagall, 1924

Marc Chagall painted this scene from an upstairs window. It looks out over some seaside houses in the **middle ground.** In the background there is a lighthouse. Because we are looking down on the landscape from above, we can also see rooftops. This is called a bird's eye view. Why do you think it is called that?

Looking Through Doors

Everything inside this house is painted flat against the sides of the box. This even includes the furniture. When we look through the small peepholes in the sides of the box, the objects look as though they are standing in a real space.

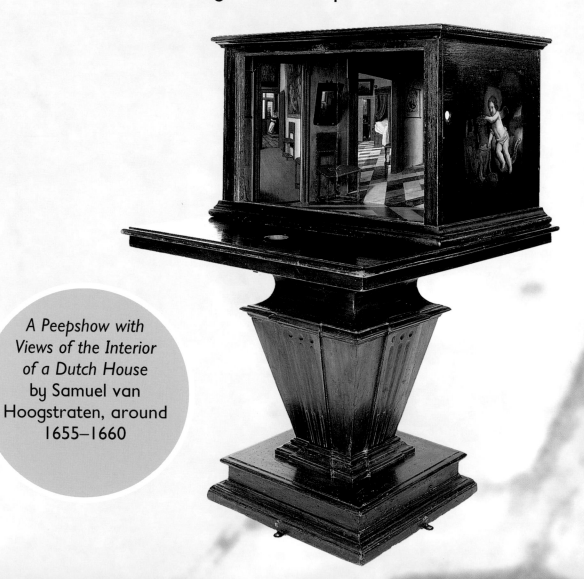

A Peepshow with Views of the Interior of a Dutch House by Samuel van Hoogstraten, around 1655–1660

Make your own viewer

You will need:

- *scissors*
- *paint*
- *glue*
- *a pencil*
- *a rectangular cardboard box, like a shoe box*
- *pictures of furniture cut out from magazines*

Instructions:

1. Cut one of the box's long sides off, so you have three walls, a ceiling, and a floor. If your box has a lid, you can probably just turn it on its side.

2. Paint the floor with a **checkered** pattern and the ceiling with one single color. Next, paint one side wall and the back wall with a wallpaper design. Finally, paint the other side wall with wallpaper and an open door leading through to another room.

3. Glue cut-out pictures of furniture against the walls. Overlap these slightly onto the floor and the corners of the walls. Finally, use the end of your scissors to make two peepholes, one on each side wall. You should now have your finished viewer!

Color and Mood

Harmony in Red (Red Room) by Henri Matisse, 1908–1909

The color of a room can affect how we feel when we are inside it. **Hot colors**, like red, make us feel warm. **Cold colors**, like blue, make a room feel cooler. Henri Matisse has named this painting of a red room *Harmony in Red* because the room looks so welcoming and cozy. What color is your bedroom? How does the color make you feel?

Vincent's Bedroom in Arles by Vincent van Gogh, about 1889

Van Gogh painted this picture of his bedroom with blue walls and orange furniture. Blue makes the room feel open and airy. The orange furniture warms the room up a bit. Blue and orange are opposite each other on the color wheel (see panel on the right). We call these colors **complementary colors** because they help each other look brighter.

Did you know?
Yellow and purple, and green and red are also complementary colors. See how they are opposite each other on the color wheel.

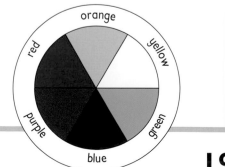

19

Murals

Some people like to paint pictures straight onto walls. We call these paintings **murals.** This **Roman** mural was painted on a bedroom wall more than 2,000 years ago. Painting a pretend view from a window would have made the room seem much larger.

Wall painting from the bedroom of a villa in a village near Pompeii, Italy, in the 1st century B.C.E.

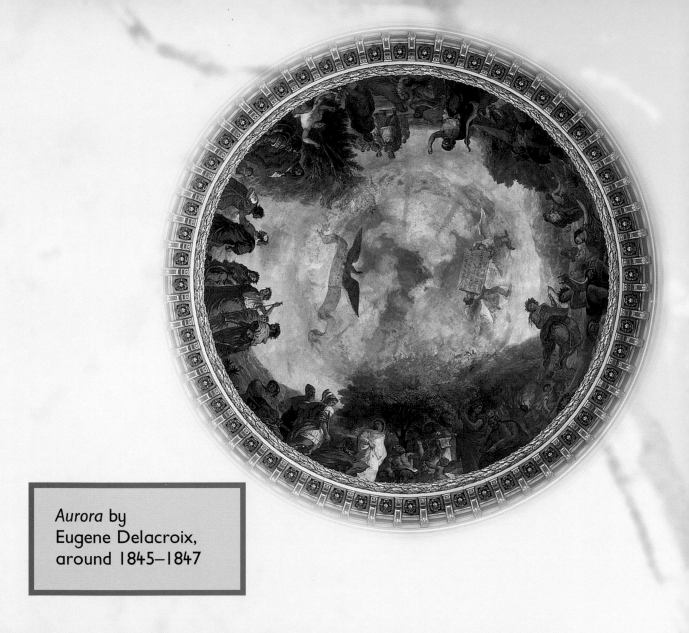

This is a ceiling mural. The artist wants us to think that the room is very high and open to the sky. Try to imagine what the room would look like with such an amazing ceiling.

Fantasy Rooms

Artist Salvador Dali is famous for creating strange works of art. Here he has designed a room to look like a famous film star's face. The curtains are her hair. The pictures on the wall are her eyes. He has made a sofa in the shape of a pair of lips and a fireplace in the shape of her nose.

The Face of Mae West by Salvador Dali, 1934–1935

Art Nouveau Interior by
Alphonse Marie Mucha

Artists around the end of the **nineteenth century**
were very interested in using patterns from nature in
their designs. This style is called **Art Nouveau.** The
fireplace in this room has been designed to look like a
tree growing out of the ground. The wall is decorated
with a peacock displaying its feathers.

Homes and Gardens

The members of this family are enjoying being in their garden on a sunny day. The water fountain and the flower pots make the garden look very grand. The artist has painted the trees and other plants in a misty, fuzzy way. It feels as though we are watching a perfect dreamlike world.

A Lady and Gentleman with Two Girls in a Garden by Nicolas Lancret, around 1742

Many people have sheds in their backyards. This is where garden tools are stored, along with many other things. This **sculpture** was once an ordinary garden shed. The artist removed all of the objects and hung them from the ceiling using clear thread, along with bits of wood from the shed. It looks as though the shed has exploded!

25

Clean Your Room!

The objects in this room tell a story about two rich but lazy people. It is a large room but it is messy. The servant, on the right, is annoyed at having to look after the owners of the house. Look at how William Hogarth has cleverly shown us another room through the archway. This makes the picture look more **three-dimensional.**

The Tête à Tête (The Breakfast Scene) by William Hogarth, 1745

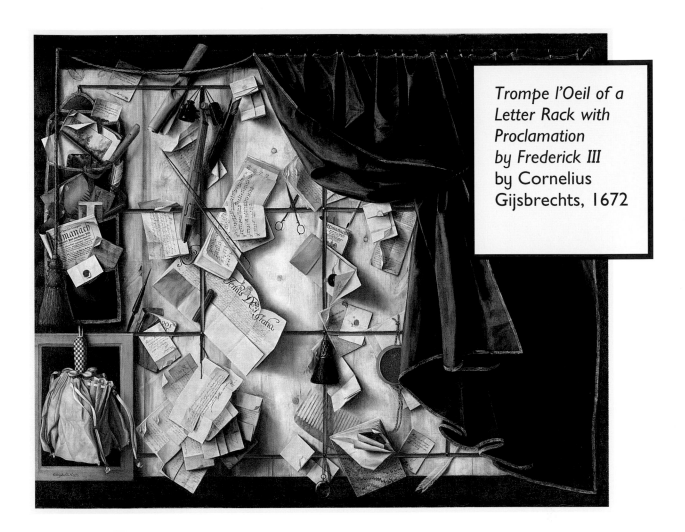

Trompe l'Oeil of a Letter Rack with Proclamation by Frederick III by Cornelius Gijsbrechts, 1672

The people in William Hogarth's picture could have used a rack like this to keep their room clean. The objects look so real you think you can touch them. But they are just a flat painting. A painted illusion like this is called a "tromp l'oeil."

Your Neighborhood

Our homes are surrounded by other homes, and the local **environment.** Robert Rauschenberg collected photographs and newspaper clippings that showed what it was like to live in his hometown. He used them to make this **collage.** Artwork that uses lots of different materials is called "mixed-media."

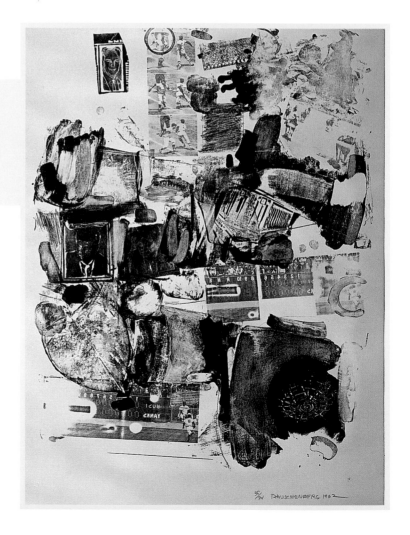

A City by Robert Rauschenberg, 1962

Make your own mixed-media collage

You will need:

- *a collection of objects that remind you of your home and neighborhood*
- *a large piece of paper*
- *glue*

Instructions:

1. Collect together some bits and pieces that remind you of your home and neighborhood. These could include:

   - photographs of buildings, rooms, and furniture cut out from magazines
   - photographs or **sketches** of family and friends
   - printouts from the Internet about your hometown
   - candy wrappers from your local store
   - photographs or sketches of your local environment
   - rubbings made with wax crayons showing **textures** you find near your house.

2. Arrange the objects you have found across a large piece of paper and glue them down.

3. You have now finished your mixed-media collage!

Glossary

architect   someone who designs buildings

Art Nouveau   style of art, architecture, and design that was popular in western Europe from the 1890s to the early 1900s

checkered   having a pattern of squares

cold color   color that makes you feel cold, like blue or green

collage   artwork made from materials glued on to a backing

complementary colors opposite colors on the color wheel

environment   surroundings in which plants, animals, and people live

fifteenth century   period of 100 years, between 1400 to 1499

hot color   color that makes you feel hot, like red, yellow, or orange

middle ground   area of a picture that is in the middle distance, between the foreground and the background

mural   painting on a wall

nineteenth century   period of 100 years, between 1800 to 1899

patchwork   pattern made by sewing many small pieces of fabric together

perspective   technique that artists use to give pictures a feeling of space and distance

plaster   fine white powder that sets hard when it is mixed with water and then left to dry

Renaissance   period of European history between the 1300s and 1500s when there was a renewed interest in art

Roman   from the period of the ancient Roman Empire

sculpture   piece of art made from a solid material

sketch   rough drawing

texture   how something feels

three-dimensional   when an object has height, width, and depth

tone   light and shade

Victorian   period of history when Queen Victoria was Queen of Great Britain, from 1837 to 1901

More Books to Read

Heinemann Library's **How Artists Use** series:

- *Color*
- *Line and Tone*
- *Pattern and Texture*
- *Perspective*
- *Shape*

Heinemann Library's **The Life and Work of** series:

- *Alexander Calder*
- *Auguste Rodin*
- *Buonarroti Michelangelo*
- *Claude Monet*
- *Diego Rivera*
- *Edgar Degas*
- *Frederick Remington*
- *Georges Seurat*
- *Grandma Moses*
- *Henri Matisse*
- *Henry Moore*
- *Joseph Turner*
- *Leonardo da Vinci*
- *Mary Cassatt*
- *Paul Cezanne*
- *Paul Gauguin*
- *Paul Klee*
- *Pieter Brueghel*
- *Rembrandt van Rijn*
- *Vincent van Gogh*
- *Wassily Kandinsky*

Index